Emotional Manipulation Tactics

35 Covert Techniques Of How Manipulators Control Personal Relationship

TESS BINDER

Copyright © 2015 Tess Binder

All rights reserved. No part of this publication may be reproduced, distributed, or transmitted in any form or by any means, including photocopying, recording, or other electronic or mechanical methods, without the prior written permission of the publisher, except in the case of brief quotations embodied in critical reviews and certain other noncommercial uses permitted by copyright law.

ISBN-13: 978-1508473893

ISBN-10: 1508473897

DEDICATION

To all those who are unhappy in their relationships.

TABLE OF CONTENT

- CHAPTER 1 1
  - Understanding Covert Emotional Manipulation 1
- CHAPTER 2 5
  - 35 Manipulation Tactics 5
- CHAPTER 3 32
  - Knowing You Are Being Manipulated & What To Do About It 32

CHAPTER 1

Understanding Covert Emotional Manipulation

"The lion does not need the whole world to fear him, only those nearest where he roams."

- A.J. Darkholme, Rise of the Morningstar

Covert emotional manipulation is a deceptive and abusive form of exercising control in relationships. It occurs when a person uses underhanded methods to change the other person's thinking, behavior and perceptions for the purpose of gaining power and control.

A manipulative relationship is unbalanced and one-sided because it advances the manipulator's goals at the expense of the one being manipulated. It lures the victims in and holds them psychologically captive. We do not easily recognize it for what it is because it goes against our basic assumptions about human behavior.

As a matter of fact, manipulation is a sign of an unhealthy personality functioning. Manipulative people do not consciously plan their maneuvers. Rather, they come from a personality disorder within them that are played out within the context of the other person who entertains the manipulator and unknowingly fuels the manipulation.

Covert emotional manipulation is sneaky and dangerous. It systematically wears away at a person's sense of self-worth, self-confidence, self-concept and personal value. It robs a person of independent judgment, soundness of mind and trust in their own perceptions. Emotional abuse is really worse than its physical form for it cuts to the very core of a person and create deeper and more lasting internal scars.

How do you know a manipulative person?

Many manipulators are spiteful, cruel and amazingly skilled at deceit. Disturbingly, they are often successful as they are usually discovered after the damage has been done. Although they are deceitful, they come across as caring, hurting, vulnerable or defending. They take advantage of our weakness and better qualities as well with the sole objective of gaining the upper hand.

Manipulative people may appear strong and self- confident but inwardly they often nurse feelings of insecurity. On the surface, they are benevolent, friendly or flattering. They are confident, relaxed and seldom anxious. They are naturally good at reading non-verbal signals and as a result appear to be empathetic, a false characteristic which endears us to them. We think they have our best interest at heart but the goal is just power and nothing else. They deny that their motives are self-serving and ruthlessly pursue their objectives at other people's cost.

We do not realize what is going on while we are being manipulated because our negative emotions usually affect our judgment or perception. It's even harder for someone who grew up being manipulated to discern what's going on due to its familiarity. The manipulator may use pleasant words or words that play on your sympathy and guilt to override your instincts. He is also an impromptu actor. He knows just when to shed a tear to suit his needs or lose himself in a fit of rage.

A psychopathic manipulator needs to satisfy his need for power and control. Manipulators with narcissistic personality disorder manipulate to satisfy their need for approval, admiration and attention. Even people without serious psychological disorders occasionally use manipulation to get what they want as well. They do not care about how their pursuit for personal gain may affect the other person. They are willing to go all out to attain their goal. Deception constitutes a very entertaining game for them.

Your best defense is to study their tactics so you could be prepared to identify them for what they really are. This way, you will be better prepared to protect yourself from abuse and exploitation, set limitations and make sound decisions about who you keep in your live. That said, the 35 covert emotional manipulation tactics that follows will be of tremendous help.

CHAPTER 2

35 Manipulation Tactics

Love Bombing

This is a tactic designed to influence a person by a superfluous show of affection and attention. Also known as positive reinforcement, it is a preliminary tactic used to hook a person more deeply to the relationship. Flattery, praise, gifts, attention, adoration, intense sex and appreciation are some common tools used. Others include constant texting, superficial sympathy, profuse apologies, public recognition and public acknowledgement in the presence of family and friends

There will be no evident of a negative behavior at the onset but demonstrations of excessive positive virtues intend to dazzle and put the victim in a continual ecstatic state. Ideally, most normal people you just meet do not make declarations of eternal love without really knowing you. They do not engage in excessive flattery, shed crocodile tears, praise you publicly, laugh profusely at your jokes and shower you with gifts and money. Watch out! These patterns of behavior are cause for suspicion.

"Wow, you're the most attractive woman in this room tonight!"

By continually bombarding a person with romantic encounters, declarations of once-in-a-lifetime love and flattery without any evident of negative behavior, the manipulator seeks to gain and retain the attention of the intended victim and once this is successful, the manipulator begins to unfold other deadly tactics to test their victims.

Traumatic Bonding

Having made his victim dependent on his constant praise and attention, the manipulator now begins to provide it intermittently. This tactic, also known as intermittent reinforcement, plays with the victim's feeling. One minute, there is an excessive declaration of love, then the next one will take a while coming. This makes the victim uncertain, anxious, fearful and doubtful. This phase creates a stronger bond. Why is this so?

It's simple: having been accustomed to receiving positive reinforcements that have suddenly becomes intermittent, you go through an internal turmoil. You do not know what you may be doing wrong and you fear that you may be losing him or her. Sometimes you may feel you are overreacting. You confront the manipulator about this and of course it is denied. The denials will only assure you for a while and then the withdrawal continues. The manipulator intentionally does this to make you more desperate and to increase his power over you.

The Sympathetic Approach

"hook-you-in-and-make-you-sorry-for-me"

Emotional manipulators often attempt to establish intimacy early in a relationship by sharing deep and deep personal information that is mostly untrue. They do this to bridge the trust barrier so that once they share something very private and personal with you, you will begin to feel sorry for them and see them as emotionally open, very sensitive and a little vulnerable. The information they share will be relevant to you. Watch out! It is a tactic to get you to trust them and equally confide something very personal. Eventually, they will use the personal information you shared with them to hurt or manipulate you.

Negative Reinforcement

This is the reward or incentive a manipulator offers for the removal of an action he finds undesirable. Thus, when you do want the manipulator wants, he stops performing the negative behavior, e.g., coming home late. In the future, if you want your partner to come home early etc, you will do what you did the first time. What this means is that you are being conditioned through the negative reinforcers the manipulator deliberately introduces.

Blame The Victim

It is never an emotional manipulator's fault as they will almost never accept blame for anything. They may pin the blame on someone else or even you. It is difficult being straightforward with them because you eventually take the blame. How they do this is to turn statements that you innocently make against you and make you the problem. They play the blame game with expertise.

If you say, "I am so angry right now. How could you forget my birthday?"

The response, "I feel so sad that you will think that I will intentionally forget your birthday. If only you could understand the great personal stress that I am going through all this while but didn't want to bother you with. You are right though, maybe I should have put aside my pain and focus on your birthday. I'm really so sorry about that."

If despite this explanation, you express reservations at being made to accept the guilt for the situation or still insist what was said or done deeply hurt your feelings, the manipulator will resort to anger or aggression.

The covert aggressive manipulator may say: "You are always making me do things that you want to do. I never even get to do anything that I like!" or "you drove me to it!"

The more aggressive one will brandish anger, "now are really starting to piss me off!"

This tactic is effective as it deflects your hurt and anger. It makes you start to consider the role of the other person in the situation and you begin to conclude that he or she may not entirely be at fault. You feel you are too harsh and so you back down.

The Crazy Making Tactics

Also called gaslighting, this sophisticated manipulative tactic is aimed at challenging the intended victim's sense of reality by creating loads of doubt in their minds. The result is that the victim begins to distrust their own judgments about issues.

This is done in two ways:

I.   An unwavering and vehement denial with a display of righteous indignation. The denial that comes with a statement you are certain was made will be so convincingly expressed that you will start to doubt your sanity in your quiet moments. For instance, you know he said he will pay for half the groceries. You remember clearly because you were happy it. Now he denies it so vigorously, firmly and innocently that you are left in wonder.

II.   Assertions with such a clear intensity of conviction that the victim begins to doubt their own perspective and starts to accept the manipulator's assertions as accurate. The manipulator may bring up historical facts that to a large extent seem accurate but these facts contain some distortions which are hard to prove. Nevertheless, they will be used to "ascertain" the correctness of the manipulator's position.

This tactic is a 'crazy- making one' because it creates doubts in the minds of others and increases power and control over them. Manipulators use it to conceal their malicious intent while at the same time prompting their intended victim to accede to their desires.

Withholding/ Silent Treatment

Withholding also called the silent treatment, involves holding back communication, positive feedback, response, acknowledgement, agreement and acceptance in order to punish the other person and to maintain control. Manipulators who use it as an effective tactic may accompany it with disapproving facial expressions and body language just to find out how long you can hold up before you crack.

However, this tactic is recognizable and can be addressed. If you find yourself in this position, tell the manipulator that you know you are being given the silent treatment but you are choosing this time around not to let it bother you. Tell him/ her that you are open to talk things out should he decide to talk. Afterwards, you should go about your life and with your one-sided conversations politely. Act like it's no big deal. Eventually, the issue will be resolved but you can be sure that the silent treatment will not be used as an effective tactic because it wouldn't work anymore.

Denial

This is a deliberate refusal by the aggressor to admit a wrongdoing when it is obvious to you that they have. This denial is not to be confused as the type expressed by a person who has just lost a loved one and is unable to accept and bear with the reality of this loss. The denial that accompanies a loss is usually an unconscious one because the reality is just too painful to bear. On the other hand, this particular one is an intentional manipulative maneuver by the aggressor to get others to back down, back off, or even feel guilty themselves for hinting that he is doing something wrong.

Manipulators frequently use the denial tactic to feign innocence. Statements such as, 'Who... Me?' are common. They will not admit their wrongdoing neither will they want to reflect on any role their behavior patterns have played in generating problems in their lives. Thus, they lie to themselves and those around them about their malicious intentions and acts in order to get others off their back. The success of the manipulation depends on the level of conviction and force of the denial.

You can be sure that this manipulative person is not about to change. This is because anyone who refuses to admit his wrongs in the first place will not feel any inclination to address them. By engaging in habitual denial, they are able to resist internalizing the values that can make them more responsible individuals.

Nonchalance

Manipulators use this tactic by playing dumb, actively ignoring the warnings, pleas or wishes of others as well as a general refusal to pay attention to everything and anything that might distract them from pursuing their own agenda. Often, the aggressor knows full well what you want from him when he starts to exhibit this "I don't care!" behavior. By using this tactic, he actively resists submitting himself to the tasks of paying attention to or refraining from the behavior you want him to change.

The Negative Out-doer

You can never outshine an emotional manipulator. They negate your statements by outdoing you. If you have a headache, they will have a brain tumor! They have a way of turning conversations around and putting the spotlight back on themselves.

Oh! The emotional manipulator knows all about your situation as he has been there before or even currently there – but only ten times worse! You may start to say you have had a rough day at work but you are curtly interrupted and made to listen to an account of their exceeding rougher day, making yours seem like nothing.

When this happens, they become the focus of attention and you are unable to feel any form of validation. The aim is to gain the upper hand by distancing themselves from you. The good thing is that it is easy to spot by the watchful even after frequent denials.

Charm &Empty Words

The manipulator can use charm and empty words to gain mastery over you. They tell you just what you will like to hear using empty words that are backed up by nothing in order to gain incredible power over you. "You're so special to me," or "I love you," means nothing to him but it helps to fill your need for reassurance, approval and validation.

They also use charm to mesmerize and distract you from what they are really saying by stroking your arm or hair, giving you a loving look, punctuating their speech with caresses, kisses and tender words.

The Victim Player

Emotional manipulators portray themselves as innocent victims of circumstances or someone else's behavior. They do this to elicit sympathy and evoke compassion. If you are someone who is sympathetic towards suffering, the manipulator will capitalize on your sympathy by convincing you that they are suffering in some way. You, on your own part will attempt to relieve them off their distress and this action opens you up.

They play on people's emotions (either of their partner or outsiders) by playing the role of victim. If they sense that you respond to guilt easily, then the tactics will be to try to make you feel guilty. For instance, they will say "I feel embarrassed for you whenever I see you play with Annie's kids as though they were ours – and it's all because you've never had children".

They may also solicit sympathy from other people around them such as neighbors, coworkers and friends so that it becomes easier for them to successfully manipulate their target. This way, they also get to escape condemnation or harsh judgment they may fear from others. They can also divert attention away from their actions by claiming that such action was justified based on the victim's s bad behavior.

Even when you express anger at what they have done, it is still your fault 'as you cannot control your emotions'. They find it difficult to bluntly express their emotions so they do so by covertly playing on other people's emotion in order to get their way.

Diversion

It is hard to hit a moving object. Similarly, it is hard to keep an experienced manipulator focused on a single topic of discussion without the fear of diversion. This person knows just when to change the subject when conversations become unfavorable for him. He may go round and round in circles, lie or talk about something else entirely. He may even use flattery like saying how sexy your voice sounds or how beautiful you look when being serious. The aim is to distract you and make you forget your original question.

Evasion

Closely related to diversion is the evasion technique. Manipulators can be very evasive. Ask them a specific question and they will answer in general terms. Sometimes they will give an unclear, irrelevant and rambling response. They may talk about men, women, humanity or whatever crosses their mind to steer the focus from them and their actions.

Emotional manipulators effectively use these two tactics to keep the focus off their behavior, steer us off-track, and keep themselves free of interference to promote their hidden self-serving agendas.

Lying By Omission

This is a form of lying where some truth is deliberately omitted if the person finds it inconveniencing. It is a subtle and effective technique used by very skilled manipulators to manage your impression of them and the result of their manipulation. Generally, you will be told facts that are mostly true. However, an essential detail that would make a difference to the entire fact or shed a new light to the reality of the situation will be left out. For instance, the manipulator may not tell you s/he is married. They only paint the picture they wish for you to see.

The Fear-Then-Relief Tactics

The emotional manipulator deliberately places his victim in a state of fear, quickly removes the threat and then replaces it with a mild demand for compliance. While this fear is being created, the victim goes through a lot of stress or anxiety and then it abruptly comes to an end. This sudden mood change disarms the person, making him or her unable to make rational or reasonable decision.

A manipulator wanting to go on a date with a busy career woman might say: "I know it must be pretty hard to meet people when you are working and putting a lot into your career. I understand. There are several women in my company like that who ended up alone with cats as companion… my friends and I will be going for a really cool party. You are welcome to join us, if you want to"

This is commonly expressed in everyday life as well: a bad manager who hints that your job is on the line later changes his mind and then asks you work overtime. This is a subtle offer you are likely to embrace with relief.

Disguised Questions

Manipulators hate asking questions for they feel it may make them lose control. Instead, they disguise their questions as statements. For examples: "I wish you could...", "I suppose you are going to...", "I am wondering why you..."

Deal with this by working on recognizing the difference between a direct question and a disguised question. Force the manipulator to admit it was a question by repeating the statement back to him or her. Once clarified, answer only a direct question.

Emotional Blackmail

Emotional blackmail is a system of punishments and threats that manipulators use when their initial requests or suggestions are denied. They might bring up something about your past that makes you feel guilty or ashamed. This they use as leverage to shame or threaten you, for instance, "I'll let the kids know about xyz if you do xyz."

Victims of blackmailers have a tendency to experience the feelings of fear, obligation and guilt. You fear because you are afraid to offend the manipulator. You feel obligated to fulfill his or her terms and guilty enough to comply. It is really a form of controlled anger used to systematically control a person.

Belittling Your Opinions

Manipulators intentionally belittle the opinion of others. No matter how great you think your ideas are, they won't count much to the manipulator. Your opinions do not matter. He may use words or he may do this covertly through non-verbal signs such as smug smiles, eye-rolls and scoffs. The manipulative blackmailer also knows how to belittle you using the shame and guilt that you feel. Accusations such as "You are selfish" or "you don't really care about me," are common examples.

Foot-in-the-Door Tactics

Foot-in-the-Door Tactics is executed by encouraging a small sacrifice or gift, which creates a bond that could be exploited to extract more weighty compliance. This manipulation technique is so subtle, tricky and simple it can downright be labeled as evil. You are asked to do something easy and simple and after it is done, you are asked to do the bigger task. By getting you to concede to the first request, you are likely to concede to the second one as well.

"Can I use your car to go to the store?" then the real request "Can I borrow it for the weekend?"

The principle behind it is that a small agreement establishes a bond between the manipulator and the victim. In most cases, the victim may only have agreed due to the triviality of the request or out of politeness. The more he or she goes along with minor requests or commitments, the higher the chances of continual concession along that particular subject even when the requests become larger. It's harder to say no, once you've a said yes already.

This tactic works because we want to be consistent. We justify our agreement by convincing ourselves that our initial action was borne out of genuine interest in the subject. With extensions of the first request, we feel we need to act consistently with that inner rationalization. If the manipulator had made its target and real request at once, it is likely to be refused but by using this subtle tactic, there is a very high chance of acceptance or compliance.

Another angle to this is to do something nice and then immediately ask for something in return.. "I made dinner! Oh, and honey can you do all my laundry while I watch TV?"

Trivialization

This tactic is a unique form of denial along with rationalization. It involves trivializing the significance of an emotion or event. Here, the manipulator tries to assert that his wrongdoing or behavior isn't really as irresponsible or harmful as being claimed. While he may admit part of actions was wrong (usually the inconsequential part), he will downplay the most serious one to make himself appear less guilty or downright innocent.

"…And I invited my friends over without informing you first, so what? It's not like we drank and smoked anything!"

Again, "It was just sex, nothing more", the manipulative cheater may say upon being discovered.

Through this tactic, the manipulator seeks to manage the impression others think of him. Once he can get them to think he's not such bad a person, he is still in control.

Disguised Aggression

Emotional manipulators want to be seen as good people even when they are not. So when they need to take a negative action like criticism, shifting blame or yelling at their target, they do so in disguise. While they wouldn't call you names because that would be obvious and direct, they disguise their aggression and do so indirectly. For instance, they wouldn't use an angry tone of voice instead they will lower their voice and disguise the abuse as giving advice, helping, offering solutions or teaching. On the surface, this may seem like a sincere attempt to assist. However, it's really an attempt to put you down, humiliate and control you.

Not Giving Room For Negative Emotions

This tactic involves chastising the victim for emotional behavior and ignoring the cause. By focusing on the emotional upset displayed by the victim, the manipulator conveniently shifts the attention away from him to the emotions which he claims is unacceptable.

Suddenly the issue at hand is no longer important but her emotion which needs to be worked on. He may refuse to discuss any further until she works on this emotion. He may go ahead to display the silent treatment. As a result, the victim feels frustrated at being unable to express feelings and thoughts.

Lying

Lying is an effective form of manipulation. It gives the manipulative person a superior position since they know what they are doing while you do not. Honesty will create a level playing field which wouldn't give the manipulator control or power. Remember that the manipulator wants to always be in control and deliberate dishonesty is one great way to do this. There are numerous ways they lie, such as through vagueness, by omission and distorting the truth. They will simply say anything to get what they want.

You may even notice the disparity or disconnect in their details. Questioning them about it will not make them admit their lie; instead, they will resort to denial or victim-blaming in most cases. Watchfulness is the key here as there will be times when circumstances will attest to the untruth of a person's story.

Triangulation

This is another common covert tactic at emotional manipulation. It involves introducing another person into the dynamic of the relationship as it progresses. The manipulator may talk about ex girlfriends, a woman at work, a relative or flirt with other women in your presence. He or she may even go as far as comparing you critically to another man/ woman even if it is a complete stranger! The objective of all these is to make you jealous by knocking you off balance.

The manipulative person wants you to compete for his or her affections. Therefore, provocative statements like "He wants me back, I really don't know what to do" "I wish you'd be a little more like her," are intended to make the victim jealous insecure about his or her placement in the manipulator's life.

Anyone in a normal relationship would want to assure his partner of his trustworthiness but the manipulator acts contrary. He loves to confuse you, watch you while hurt and trouble you unnecessary.

Slander

Manipulators may also use slander to discredit other people and invalidate their claims of truth. He projects his misdeed and wrong actions upon his victims. He may malign his girlfriend or wife and then turn around to say that it was their faults or wrongful actions that caused his relationship to fail.

Manipulators are masters at deception. They use one person to lie to the other and then use these two people to lie to a third. The will place distance among the people they deliberately misinform to prevent them from coming together and discovering the deception. Usually, they mix some part of the truth with the lies so that if they are caught, they can focus on that little bit of truth.

Justification

Justification or rationalization is the excuse a manipulator tries to provide for engaging in an inappropriate behavior. The manipulator uses this tactic to convince you that he is justified in the actions carried out. He makes explanations for actions that make just enough sense to convince any reasonable person.

This tactic works because the internal resistance the manipulator may have about an action or its consequence is removed, leaving him with a feeling of justification. He also manages to keep others off his back. As a result, he is at liberty to pursue his goals without external resistance and interference.

Leveling

This is a tricky manipulation tactic that attempts to put the manipulator on the same moral standing as others. It is the "you aren't perfect either" accusation thrown at the victim whenever they are confronted about an inappropriate behavior.

For instance, a woman says: "I wish you would let me know why you're upset with me instead of giving me the silent treatment and ignoring me. I do not do that. I always tell you why and when I'm upset with you."

Responds: "So you're better than me, right, isn't that what you're really saying?"

He actually means that they are two people who are equal in character so the woman's confrontational action is seen as arrogant and demanding. She will begin to wonder if she has treated him unjustly and then draws back.

This tactic works when the manipulator is resolute in his belief that that all values and behavior standards are equal if genuinely felt. By this assertion, the other person finds it hard to challenge what they deeply believe is bad behavior. The manipulator sets her own rules for her. After a while, the victim loses his own sense of values and principles.

Being Your Servant

The manipulator masks his behavior as nurturing, positive, and caring by acting as your servant and claiming to do things for your good or for the general good of the society. Manipulators who say they have your best interest at heart while they do things for you make it difficult for you to fault their bad behavior. An example of this is a wife who continually pushes her husband to take a promotion he doesn't like or feel inclined to. The wife claims it is to create a higher living standard for the children and family but the reluctant husband isn't happy about it. Since he cannot actually pinpoint the fault in her claims, he will eventually accept her rationalization of the situation but will still feel bad that he hates his new job. This tactic is difficult to recognize because on the surface it is servitude but underneath the primary aim is dominance.

Saying Yes and Meaning No

A manipulative person gives assent to get you to back down during a disagreement with no intention of changing their point of view. In a normal relationship, a person will change his stance when they begin to see the other's point.

The opposite is the case in a manipulative relationship; they will agree with you but have no intention of yielding.

Brandishing Anger

This is when the manipulator feigns intense anger to shock others into submission. Also called 'Traumatic one-trial learning,' the purpose of this brazen anger act is to avoid revealing the truth, avoid confrontation or to hide intent. The manipulator puts on this act to get what he wants. He frightens you with anger so as to make you sacrifice your desires and wants. Even if you are strong enough to resist his anger, he may switch to much lighter or joyful mood unexpectedly; this makes you so relieved you want to agree to the next request that is made.

Anger is his way of covertly training you to avoid confrontation and be subservient. You wouldn't want to confront, contradict and upset him while he displays this feigned or exaggerated anger.

The Subtle Dirty Fighter

Manipulators cannot deal with things directly. They find it hard to express their emotions directly so they will put others in a position of telling you what they wouldn't say themselves. As passive aggressors, they will talk behind your back and even if they were to tell you things directly, they will do so in subtle ways, taking from both sides of their mouth.

For instance, they will tell you sweetly that they will support you if you do go back to school. Then on the exam night while you are sitting studying at the table and their buddies show up for a poker game, the kids are upset, the TV is on full blast and the dog needs walking and they are sitting down doing nothing. The response you are likely to hear if you call "well, honey, you can't really expect life to stop just because you have an exam, can you?"

Manipulators may talk behind your back, push others to confront you and then come in to support you while placing the blame on other people. Also, they make personal statements and pretend it someone else's, for example, "everyone thinks you...","They said you...". Deal with this last tactic by asking directly for the manipulator's own opinion.

The (un)Willing Helper

Manipulators do not say no when asked to do something. In fact, they respond in the affirmative almost immediately but this is the problem: they proceed to carry out the action amidst some non- verbal signs such as heavy sighs, an annoyed facial expression or rolling eyes that says the exact opposite. When you do notice and point out that it seem they really do not want to do the task requested, they will turn around to vehemently deny it and then make you the problem as you are being 'unreasonable'.

Feigning Confusion

Covert emotional manipulators pretend to be confused about important issues brought before them. They play dumb to indicate that do not know what the other person is talking about. So you become confused and may start to doubt your own accuracy of perception. In some cases, manipulators bring in cohorts to support their story.

False Guilt

Emotional manipulators are skilled at playing the guilt card. They know that people have very different consciences than they do so they use what they know to be their victim's greater conscientiousness to keep them anxious, doubtful and submissive. They know how to make you feel guilty for your actions or inactions, for speaking up or not speaking up. "How could you think that of me??!" they will often ask. "You could never do...", "If you loved me..." etc. To a manipulator, anything is open to guilt or can be used as guilt. All a manipulator has to do is suggest to the conscientious person that they don't care enough, are too selfish, etc., and that person immediately starts to feel bad and will do whatever it takes to lessen the feelings of guilt.

What you can do is to minimize your exposure to such guilty statements. Ignore manipulative words and do not respond to them.

Shaming

Covert-aggressive manipulators use shaming to make others feel unworthy or inadequate. They use subtle sarcasm, rhetorical comments, a fierce look, an unpleasant tone of voice amongst others to increase fear in their victim, make them unsure of themselves and defer to them. This shame is associated with false condemnation made by the aggressor for the purpose of maintaining a position of dominance.

CHAPTER 3

Knowing You Are Being Manipulated & What To Do About It

How To Know You Are Being Manipulated

<u>Anxiety</u>: You feel anxious each time your partner is about to request for a favor. You are afraid they may ask you do what you don't want to do yet you know you cannot refuse their request.

<u>Mood</u>: Your mood fully depends on the state of the relationship.

<u>You End Up Apologizing</u>: You always end up apologizing because what you say is always misinterpreted.

<u>Your Relationship Feel Very Complex</u>: you even find it hard to explain your relationship to friends and family, telling them that it's just "complicated".

You Hate Yourself: You know you are weak and you hate yourself for it. You have the feeling your partner is taking advantage of your generosity and niceness but you're too weak to challenge them about it.

You Justify Your Actions: You find yourself justifying your actions every time and still end up convincing yourself that it is you who do these favor freely without being manipulated.

Inadequacy: you always think you need to improve yourself in some way such as your personality, body, career etc. you keep asking your partner if there is something wrong.

A Word Is No Longer Enough: a simple no or yes is no longer enough. You find yourself using plenty of words to explain simple actions you take. You strive to make your partner understand the reasons behind your decisions. Meanwhile, your partner is always vague and doesn't see the need to justify his actions.

Expectations Grow: Your partner wants more from you every time. No matter what you do or how much love you show, they keep asking for more.

<u>You Can't Lie Anymore</u>: You just cannot lie to your manipulator even when it is an innocent lie and you will never get caught. Simple lies such as telling them you are busy so you could have time for yourself becomes an impossible task.

<u>You feel guilty</u>: You think you are not being a good person and that it's your entire fault. Even while you are relaxed and idle, you feel guilty that you aren't using that time to please them in some way.

<u>Obligations</u>: You feel you owe them for loving you or for being in your life. You constantly feel grateful and obligated to them.

<u>Thoughts Of Selfishness</u>: You think you may be selfish for not assisting them in their troubles. Each time you turn down their request, you feel so bad that you may even find it hard to look them in the eyes!

<u>Inability To Say No</u>: you find it hard to say no to them. It's virtually impossible even if it is the right thing to do.

Others include: you question your sanity, you are berated for doing things you enjoy and you find yourself always planning your life around their schedule.

Dealing With Manipulation

Stay connected to your larger social circles. Manipulators cannot work effectively if you are surrounded by family and friends as they would want to pull you away in isolation.

Meditate and spend time to know your own thoughts and well-thought out judgments.

Be Aware: Take time to spot the tactics mentioned above.

Recognize your own emotions within the relationship. Define it and understand the pattern.

Listen to your feelings. Are you feeling confused or full of self-doubt? Pay close attention to your partner's words and actions.

Assess Your Relationship. Consider how a direct confrontation may turn out. Will it be worth it? You might want to talk with close friends first.

Having recognize some of these subtle emotional manipulations, point it out at the point it occurs. Do it calmly and assertively, for instance, "I feel that you are trying to manipulate me here but I choose not to go with it...I would prefer a healthy interaction between us".

Confront them. The manipulator will rarely just admit it, particularly if you are acting nervous. Point out the behaviors that are worrisome. Request for a change of such behaviors, keep your cool if they deny or minimize.

Get support. Discuss with your doctor or someone who understands Personality Disorders. Talk to a trusted friend, a close family and in extreme fearful situations, the police.

Terminate the contact if necessary then immediately. Keep company with people who value you and treat you with respect and honor.

Made in the USA
San Bernardino, CA
04 November 2016